HALF BREED

NATASHA MARSHALL

SAMUEL FRENCH

samuelfrench.co.uk

Soho Theatre and **Talawa Theatre Company** present

HALF BREED

Written and performed by **Natasha Marshall**

DIRECTOR
Miranda Cromwell

SET AND COSTUME DESIGNER
Ruby Spencer Pugh

LIGHTING DESIGNER
Amy Mae

SOUND DESIGNER
Xana

STAGE MANAGER
Rosie Giarratana

Half Breed was first performed at **The Box, Assembly** at the Edinburgh Festival Fringe 2017 before its London premiere at **Soho Theatre** on Monday 11 September.

This script went to press during rehearsals, and may differ from the text in performance.

Cast

NATASHA MARSHALL *Writer and Performer*
Growing up mixed-race in the West Country, Natasha has enjoyed performing from a young age. At eighteen she decided to move to London to pursue her acting dreams and attend East15 acting school. During the course Natasha discovered her love for poetry and started writing. After graduating in 2012, Natasha moved back and forth between London and the West Country, but would perform her poems at open mic nights for spoken word in London. Natasha then went on to participate in Royal Court Writers Group (2014/2015), before moving back to London permanently to attend the BBC Comedy Room, BBC Sketch Group and BBC London Voices (2016), Soho Theatre's Writers' Lab, Soho Rising (2016) and Talawa Firsts (2016).

Creative Team

MIRANDA CROMWELL *Director*

Miranda Cromwell is a freelance director and artistic director of Twisted Theatre. Trained at National Theatre Studio Directors course 2015. Previously Young Company director at Bristol Old Vic. Directing credits include; *The Rest Of Your Life* (The Bush Theatre); *FEED* (Company 3); *Magic Elves* (Bristol Old Vic); *Death and Treason* (Twisted Theatre, RSW tour); *Dancing at Lughnasa* (Charleston College of Arts, USA); *Pigeon English* (Edinburgh Fringe Festival, Underbelly); *Children of Killers* (Cottesloe, National Theatre); *Our Country's Good* (BOV Young Company, NSDF, received the judges award for artistic leadership). Other credits include: staff director on *Angels in America* (National Theatre) and associate director on *Coram Boy* (Bristol Old Vic).

RUBY SPENCER PUGH *Set and Costume Designer*

Ruby is a set and costume designer for theatre, film, and festivals. Ruby trained at Royal Welsh College of Music and Drama where she won the Philip and Christine Carne Prize for gaining the highest mark. Ruby has collaborated on a variety of projects from adaptions of classic texts to devised theatre. Ruby is Artistic Director of Twisted Theatre. Design credits include; *A Spark and A Beating Heart* (Firebird Theatre); *Mental* (Vault Festival); *Little Tim and the Brave Sea Captain* (The Wardrobe Ensemble, Bristol Old Vic); *Then Again* (Tremolo Theatre); *The Love of the Nightingale* (Bristol Old Vic YC) and *Magic Elves* (Bristol Old Vic).

AMY MAE *Lighting Designer*

Amy works across Theatre, Dance, Site Specific and Devised performance. She trained at RADA on the postgraduate Stage Electrics and Lighting Design course and has a degree in Stage Management and Performing Arts from the University of Winchester. Amy designed the lighting for the acclaimed 'Pie Shop' version of *Sweeney Todd* which is currently playing at the Barrow Street Theatre in New York. She won the Knight of Illumination Award in 2015 for the London production, and her design for the New York production has been nominated for the 2017 Drama Desk Award for Outstanding Lighting Design and the Lucille Lortel Award for Best Lighting Design. Recent credits include: *The Ugly One* (Park Theatre); *Babette's Feast* (The Print Room); *The Lounge* (Soho Theatre); *Start Swimming* (Young Vic); *Wordsworth* (Theatre By The Lake); *Paradise Of The Assassins* (Tara Theatre); *Knife Edge* (Pond Restaurant, Dalston); *Minaturists 55* (Arcola Theatre); *Prize Fights* (Royal Academy of Dramatic Art); *Orphans* (Southwark Playhouse); *Macbeth* (Italia Conti); *I'm Not Here Right Now* (Paines Plough's Roundabout and Soho Theatre); *Liola* (New Diorama Theatre); *Children In Uniform*; *Punk Rock* (Tristan Bates Theatre); *Sweeney Todd* (Harringtons Pie and Mash Shop and West End); *The Three*

Sisters (Cockpit Theatre); *Cat Couture* (Music Video); *In Bed* (London Theatre Workshop); *Henry V* (Royal Academy of Dramatic Art); *Pool, The Gut Girls* (Brockley Jack Theatre); *The Legacy* (The Place). She was one of the invited speakers at the 2017 Showlight Conference in Florence. http://www.amymaelighting.com

XANA *Sound Designer*

Xana is a multidisciplinary live loop musician, composer, poet, sound designer and installation artist who creates inter-genre soundscapes through beatbox, vocal looping, coding, archive material, freestyle poetry and field recordings. Xana also works as a community organiser working with SEND (Special Educational Need and Disabilities) and EBD (Educational Behavioural Difficulties) children and young adults, within sound and will be one of the artist-in-residence this October (17/18) in the learning departments at Tate Britain and Tate Modern. Theatre credits include: *Salt* by Selina Thompson (Mayfest Arnolfini, Bristol/Yorkshire Festival, Leeds), Afrofuturistic Pit Party (Barbican); *We Raise Our Hands In the Sanctuary* (Albany Theatre), *Untitled* by Somalia Seaton (Company 3), *Sweet Like Chocolate Boy* by Tristan Fynn-Aiduenu (Cockpit Theatre), *Primetime* (Royal Court Theatre). Film credits: *the ancestors came* directed by Cecile Emeke, *How was your day* directed by Tal Iungman.

ROSIE GIARRATANA *Stage Manager*

Rosie is a freelance stage manager based in Bristol. Having initially trained as a sign language interpreter, she enjoys working with Deaf theatre companies and a diverse range of companies and artists. Recent projects include: *The Who's Tommy* (Ramps on the Moon); *The House of Bernarda Alba* (Manchester Royal Exchange/Graeae); *Blue Heart* (Tobacco Factory Theatres/Orange Tree Theatre); *Monster Raving Loony* (Plymouth Theatre Royal); *The Solid Life of Sugar Water* (Plymouth Theatre Royal/Graeae); *Under a Cardboard Sea* (Bristol Old Vic Young Company); *Lost & Found* (Gloucester Dance) and *Grounded* (Deafinitely Theatre).

Soho Theatre is London's most vibrant venue for new theatre, comedy and cabaret. We occupy a unique and vital place in the British cultural landscape. Our mission is to produce new work, discover and nurture new writers and artists, and target and develop new audiences. We work with artists in a variety of ways, from full producing of new plays, to co-producing new work, working with associate artists and presenting the best new emerging theatre companies that we can find.

We have numerous artists on attachment and under commission, including Soho Six and a thriving Young Company of writers and comedy groups. We read and see hundreds of scripts and shows a year.

'the place was buzzing, and there were queues all over the building as audiences waited to go into one or other of the venue's spaces....young, exuberant and clearly anticipating a good time.' Guardian.

We attract over 240,000 audience members a year at Soho Theatre, at festivals and through our national and international touring. We produced, co-produced or staged over 35 new plays in the last 12 months.

As an entrepreneurial charity and social enterprise, we have created an innovative and sustainable business model. We maximise value from Arts Council England and philanthropic funding, contributing more to government in tax and NI than we receive in public funding.

Registered Charity No: 267234

Soho Theatre, 21 Dean Street
London W1D 3NE
Admin 020 7287 5060
Box Office 020 7478 0100

Supported using public funding by
**ARTS COUNCIL
ENGLAND**
LOTTERY FUNDED

OPPORTUNITIES FOR WRITERS AT SOHO THEATRE

We are looking for unique and unheard voices – from all backgrounds, attitudes and places.

We want to make things you've never seen before.

Alongside workshops, readings and notes sessions, there are several ways writers can connect with Soho Theatre. You can

- **enter** our prestigious biennial competition the **Verity Bargate Award** just as **Vicky Jones** did in 2013 with her Award-winning first play *The One*.

- **participate** in our nine month long **Writers' Labs programme**, where we will take you through a three-draft process.

- **submit** your script to submissions@sohotheatre.com where your play will go directly to our Artistic team

- **invite us** to see your show via coverage@sohotheatre.com

We consider every submission for production or any of the further development opportunities.

sohotheatre.com

Keep up to date:

sohotheatre.com/mailing-list
@sohotheatre all social media

DEVELOPMENT AND DONORS

Soho Theatre is a charity and social enterprise. We are supported by Arts Council England and we put every £1 we make back into our work. Our supporters are key to our success and we are immensely grateful for their support. We would like to thank Soho Theatre Friends and Members as well as our supporters:

Principal Supporters
Nicholas Allott
Hani Farsi
Jack and Linda Keenan
Amelia and Neil Mendoza
Lady Susie Sainsbury
Carolyn Ward
Jennifer and Roger Wingate

The Soho Circle
Celia Atkin
Moyra Doyle
Stephen Garrett
Hedley and Fiona Goldberg
Jon Grant
Tim Macready
Suzanne Pirret

Corporate Supporters
Adnams Southwold
Bargate Murray
Bates Wells & Braithwaite
Cameron Mackintosh Ltd
EPIC Private Equity
Financial Express
Fosters
The Groucho Club
John Lewis Oxford Street
Latham & Watkins LLP
Lionsgate UK
The Nadler Hotel
Oberon Books Ltd
Overbury Leisure
Quo Vadis
Richmond Associates
Soho Estates
Soundcraft

Trusts & Foundations
The Andor Charitable Trust
The Austin and Hope Pilkington Charitable Trust
Backstage Trust
Bertha Foundation
Boris Karloff Charitable Foundation
Bruce Wake Charitable Trust
The Buzzacott Stuart Defries Memorial Fund
The Chapman Charitable Trust
The Charles Rifkind and Jonathan Levy Charitable Settlement
Cockayne – Grants for the Arts and The London Community Foundation
The Coutts Charitable Trust
The David and Elaine Potter Foundation
The D'Oyly Carte Charitable Trust
The Ernest Cook Trust

The Edward Harvist Trust
The 8th Earl of Sandwich Memorial Trust
The Eranda Foundation
Esmée Fairbairn Foundation
The Fenton Arts Trust
The Foundation for Sport and the Arts
The Foyle Foundation
The Goldsmiths' Company
Harold Hyam Wingate Foundation
Help A London Child
Hyde Park Place Estate Charity
The Ian Mactaggart Trust
The Idlewild Trust
John Ellerman Foundation
John Lewis Oxford Street Community Matters Scheme
John Lyon's Charity
The John Thaw Foundation
JP Getty Jnr Charitable Trust
The Kobler Trust
The Mackintosh Foundation
The Mohamed S. Farsi Foundation
The Peggy Ramsay Foundation
The Rose Foundation
The Royal Victoria Hall Foundation
St Giles-in-the-Fields and William Shelton Educational Charity
The St James's Piccadilly Charity
Teale Charitable Trust
The Theatres Trust
The Thistle Trust
Unity Theatre Charitable Trust
The Wolfson Foundation

Soho Theatre Best Friends
Matthew and Brooke Barzun
Nick Bowers
Prof Dr Niels Brabandt
Barbara Broccoli
Richard Collins
David and Beverly Cox
Miranda Curtis
Norma Heyman
Isobel and Michael Holland
Beatrice Hollond
David King
Lady Caroline Mactaggart
Hannah Pierce
Amy Ricker
Ian Ritchie and Jocelyne van den Bossche
Ann Stanton
Alex Vogel
Sian and Matthew Westerman
Mark Whiteley
Gary Wilder
Alexandra Williams

Hilary and Stuart Williams

Soho Theatre Dear Friends
Nick Allan
Christiane Amanpour
Ken Anderson
David Aukin
Natalie Bakova
James Boyle
Rajan Brotia
James Brown
Simon Brown, Founder The ESTAS Group
Lisa Bryer
Steve Coogan
Fiona Dewar
Cherry and Rob Dickins
Manu Duggal
Chris Evans
Denzil and Renate Fernandez
Dominic Flynn
Jonathan Glanz and Manuela Raimondo
Alban Gordon
Kate Horton
John James
Dede Johnston
Shappi Khorsandi
Jeremy King
Lynne Kirwin
Michael Kunz
David and Linda Lakhdhir
Anita and Brook Land
Jonathan Levy
Patrick Marber
Nick Mason and Annette Lynton Mason
Aoife O'Brien
Adam Morley
Aoife O'Brien
Rick Pappas
Natasha Parker
Leanne Pollock
Lauren Prakke
Phil and Jane Radcliff
John Reid
James Robertson
Sue Robertson
Alexandra Sears
Robert & Melanie Stoutzker
Dominic and Ali Wallis
Garry Watts
Gregg Wilson
Andrea Wong
Matt Woodford
Henry Wyndham
Christopher Yu

Soho Theatre Good Friends
Oladipo Agboluaje
James Atkinson
Jonathan and Amanda Baines
Uri Baruchin
Antonio Batista
Alex Bridport
Jesse Buckle
Indigo Carnie

Paul Carpenter
Chris Carter
Sharon Eva Degen
Michelle Dietz
Niki di Palma
Jeff Dormer
Geoffrey and Janet Eagland
Edwina Ellis
Peter Fenwick
Gail and Michael Flesch
Sue Fletcher
Daniel and Joanna Friel
James Flitton
Cyrus Gilbert-Rolfe
Doug Hawkins
Etan Ilfeld
John Ireland
Fran Jones
Susie Lea
Simon Lee
Tom Levi
Ian Livingston
Nicola Martin
Kathryn Marten
Amanda Mason
Neil Mastrarrigo
Robert McFarland
Gerry McGrail
Andrew and Jane McManus
Mr and Mrs Roger Myddelton
Dr Tara Naidoo
Max Nicholson
Alan Pardoe
Edward Pivcevic
Sadia Quyam
Stephanie Ressort
Barry Serjent
Ed Smith
Hari Sriskantha
Francis and Marie-Claude Stobart
Sam Swallow
Lesley Symons
Sue Terry
Gabriel Vogt
Anja Weise
Mike Welsh
Matt Whitehurst
Allan Willis
Liz Young

Soho Theatre has the support of the Channel 4 Playwrights' Scheme sponsored by Channel 4 Television.

Also kindly supported by Westminster City Council West End Ward Budget and the London Borough of Waltham Forest.

We would also like to thank those supporters who wish to remain anonymous.

This list is correct as of July 2017.

Talawa Theatre Company
30 years of celebrating Black theatre

'I believe theatre is vital to our lives, it's important to see oneself reflected in the arts, and at Talawa this is our aim.'
Michael Buffong, Artistic Director, Talawa Theatre Company

Talawa is the UK's primary Black led theatre company. Talawa has mounted more than fifty productions over our thirty year history, recent productions have included the critically acclaimed production of *King Lear* by William Shakespeare (co-production with the Royal Exchange Theatre, in association with Birmingham Repertory Theatre), *Girls* by Theresa Ikoko (co-production with Soho Theatre and HighTide), *All My Sons* by Arthur Miller (Royal Exchange Theatre, UK tour), *Moon on a Rainbow Shawl* by Errol John (National Theatre, UK tour) and *God's Property* by Arinze Kene (Soho Theatre, UK tour).

Talawa was founded in 1986 by Black artists and activists Yvonne Brewster OBE, Mona Hammond, Carmen Munroe and Inigo Espejel, in order to address the lack of opportunities for Black actors on British stages. The vision was to diversify the theatre industry; making it fully representative of the UK's population. Today, led by Artistic Director Michael Buffong, Talawa dedicates its resources to creating high quality touring productions and to developing Black artists. The company enables this by:

- producing one national touring production a year
- developing a canon of new Black British plays through commissioning, training and giving dramaturgical feedback through the free to use script reading service
- through our artist development programme MAKE, we support the careers of over 100 Black theatre artists, backstage staff and administrators annually by offering training, mentoring, and a chance to develop and present creative ideas
- using theatre as a learning and/or personal development tool in schools, community groups and in businesses

SUPPORT US

Talawa Theatre Company is an Arts Council England National Portfolio Organisation. and a registered charity. All the money that we earn or raise is reinvested back into the work that we do. We receive the support of trusts and foundations including Esmée Fairbairn Foundation, the John Ellerman Foundation and the Martin Bowley Charitable Trust.

Talawa was recently awarded the Catalyst Evolve fund from Arts Council England. This means that for every £1 we fundraise* the Arts Council will match it, so we will effectively double our money. With your help we can continue to tour engaging and powerful theatre for audiences across the UK and support the next generation of Black artists to create dynamic new work which reflects the UK today.

Visit us at talawa.com/support-us **to find out how you can support us**

Registered charity No 2005971

---

* ACE will match any income raised up to a total of £105,000

TALAWA THEATRE COMPANY

Artistic Director – Michael Buffong

Executive Director – Natasha Bucknor

Administrator – Mimi Findlay

Finance Manager – Zewditu Bekele

Producer, Participation & Learning – Gail Babb

Marketing and Communications Manager – Sanjit Chudha

Literary Associate – Jane Fallowfield

Make Co-ordinator – Pooja Sitpura

BOARD

Derek Brown, Heather Clark-Charrington, Greg Hersov (Chair), James Kenworth, Sue Mayo, Viloshini Sinden, and Colin Washington.

PATRONS

Nonzo Anozie and Michaela Coel

CONTACT US

Get involved at Talawa. Visit us at www.talawa.com on Twitter @TalawaTheatreCo or Instagram @talawatc or by email to hq@talawa.com

ISBN 978-0-573-11500-4

www.samuelfrench.co.uk
www.samuelfrench.com

AUTHOR'S NOTE

As an actress I found myself frustrated by the lack of diverse roles for black females. I wanted to be more than a stereotype and was constantly searching for a part that would speak the type of truth that I had come from. Not just as an actor but also as an audience member I had a yearning to see something that was coming from a different perspective on "being black" that could move my soul. I soon realised that if I don't write about it, then the voice will never be heard. I decided to create the type of theatre I wanted to see, and write a story that had been screaming inside of me for a long time. And so *Half Breed* was born.

It's a scary and liberating feeling to write this story.

It's a scary and liberating feeling to perform *Half Breed*.

Originally I thought this was just a play about being mixed-race. However after performing it, I was genuinely surprised at how many people could identify. I realised *Half Breed* is more than skin colour, it's for anyone that's ever been a misfit or on the outside looking in. It's about getting knocked down and standing up stronger and pushing through and pushing through. It's about hope.

It's based in Wiltshire and the whole village is played by Jazmin. The strength of the West Country accent varies with different characters.

ACKNOWLEDGEMENTS

Miranda Cromwell for making me see the strength in me and the strength in *Half Breed*. Steve Marmion and everyone at Soho Theatre Company, thank you for making my dreams come true and believing in me. Michael Buffong and everyone at Talawa Theatre Company, thank you for your faith and constant support in helping me reach my goals. Jane Fallowfield for your honesty and guidance – thank you. Ikenna Obiekwe at Independent Talent. I am also hugely appreciative of their programs which seek out raw and new talent, such as Soho Young Writers Lab, Soho Rising and Talawa Firsts, TYPT... Long may they continue! Thank you to the Royal Court and the Alfred Fagon award panel. Thank you to my amazing "Half Breed team". And lastly thank you to my mum and dad for basically telling the whole village about my play – thank you for supporting my dreams. It's been a group effort and I am so appreciative for everyone who contributed towards *Half Breed*, without them this wouldn't have been possible.

For my grandma
For Gemma
For anyone that can identify – this is for you

LONDON

BROGAN *(she speaks to the audience)* Do you think I'm scared...
do you ACTUALLY think I'm scared, cus I'm far from mate.
Just cus you're all together in some sort of group, in some
sort of GANG... All together, just proper staring at me.
Well I'm not intimidated...cus if you come near me right,
I will hurt you right. Cus when I lose my temper I can be
really, REALLY unreasonable. So just back up, BACK UP!
Go away, have a nice day but just go...because no, you can't
have my wallet.

Pause.

Alright now Jaz you have a go. What, you're not gunna do it?!
But I'm just showing you how to protect yourself when you
go to London. And I'm only saying this because I love you,
but if you wanna go there you just need to be more aware
of these things. At the end of the day you know me and you
know I'm not racist. I mean, I get a Chinky every Friday so
I can't be racist...but...you do need to be more aware. For
example, if you see one of "those types of people" with a big
backpack on, don't be afraid to walk away. No... No... No...
NO... That's not being judgmental, that's just being one
step ahead of the game. What? It's all in the news!!! Cus
you know like Kidulthood...well they really do act like that
in London so if they say "come on Jaz, come here 'FAM'"
or "come with us, choose a gang" just say "no thank you, I
appreciate the offer but I don't take sides and I wish you
both the best of luck for the future". Cus at the end of the day
it's too busy, too polluted, no grass, no trees, too expensive
to live in unless you're like Myleene Klass or something, so
why you wanna go? Why you wanna leave here?

JAZ Right now me and Brogan are sitting in our favourite place. Under a tree, and that might sound a bit crap like "oh that's cool, you sit with trees and chill" but Brogan took me here, way, way, way back when we first made friends.

BROGAN "This is the oldest tree in the whole woods but don't tell no one... Oh my gosh I just thought, every time we come here right, we should bring a rock to show we've been here".

JAZ I love my best friend, but that's about as spontaneous as she gets. But I have to admit that this was actually a good idea, cus seven years on and we still come here, you know like today. And now we've got tons of rocks piled high, more than I can even count and it reminds me of the tons of times we've been here. It's kinda nice.

BROGAN Hello! I said why do you wanna leave here?

JAZ I dunno... I just do.

BROGAN So let me get this straight, one last time.

JAZ *(sighs)* Again?!

BROGAN So your gran secretly put your name forward and paid this money?

JAZ Yeah...

BROGAN So that you could audition for some drama school in London?

JAZ Yeah...

BROGAN In four days' time?

JAZ Yeah...

BROGAN Bit short bloody notice isn't it!

JAZ She didn't want me to back out.

BROGAN It's never too late to back out!

JAZ Brog!

BROGAN All I'm saying is, the best thing to come out of London was EastEnders back when Tiffany was alive. But apart from that, it's nothing really that special.

BROGAN

JAZ Brogan's my best friend, white skin, blonde hair, blue eyes she's really perfect looking.

We've been best friends since year seven and she said—

BROGAN "I like your skin colour. It looks really nice because it's like you've always got a tan... So what are you then? Are you like a half-cast or something?"

JAZ She's West Country born, West Country raised, never left the county longer than a day.

BROGAN "Just don't really, wouldn't want, safer here, have a laugh, not going, never going, never never—"

JAZ Brogan's scared of pretty much anything. She's scared of getting food poisoning so she cooks it till it's burnt, it's a joke. She's scared of going uni cus she'll end up broke, scared of crashing on the motorway, cus it's too far away when its outside our village.

Hey... Brog would you come with me if I went somewhere like... I dunno, America?

BROGAN No.

JAZ Wait you're telling me you wouldn't wanna go abroad or something?

BROGAN No.

JAZ Party your life away for as long as possible?

BROGAN No.

JAZ Not have no worries?

BROGAN No.

JAZ Why?

BROGAN Because I just feel like I know what I'm good at and what I'm born to do is—

JAZ But you're seventeen!

BROGAN So?

JAZ Brogan's scared of a lot of stuff, but one thing she ain't scared of is being a mum. To be fair, I think she would be a well good one. What with her being in foster care you know? It's not like she had anyone there.

VILLAGERS Now I don't gossip, I heard from my sister-in-law's brother, she opens her legs for one after the other which implies she's bit of a—

More like a lot of a—

A right old...!

JAZ Alright, she did get about...has got about a lot.

But she don't say not one word, when people around here shout,

"Slag" and "I heard your family don't want you!"

See that's proper strong cus the only thing she ever did wrong, was search for love in the wrong places. So that's basically it, we're different but the same, outsider rejects looking in—

BROGAN —don't fit in

JAZ —don't want to.

BROGAN I got you,

JAZ I got you...

...She may not be perfect. But to me she's a blessing.

ME

JAZ So welcome to the village! I'm Jaz and I'm the only black in the village and I know I'm not "proper black" but trust me around here I'm about as black as it goes, and everyone knows.

"Yeah, it's just her and her mum, her BLACK dad did a runner before she was one".

"Yeah, sad innit, but that's what THOSE do, some women should pay more attention to the men that they screw".

"She's shit".

"Aint fit to be a mum".

"Leaving that poor old grandma to raise her child".

"No wonder her fucking child is running around wild".

BROGAN "Oi! What you saying about her gran?"

JAZ "Jus leave it Brog, leave it."

BROGAN "No, why don't they SHUT THE—"

JAZ I am that mixed-race kid, the one that's the epitome of mixed up, like 50/50, on the fence, lukewarm, in-between maybe. No seriously, even my personality's indecisive, like my brain is just as confused as my skin. Should I stay here? Or should I try move to London?

Stay. Go. Stay. Go. Stay. Go. Stay... "Go back to your own country!"

Let me tell you, right. To be a beautiful girl where I'm from, is to be the epitome of the "girl next door". So basically white, so I'm almost there but not just quite. It's a frustrating place to be in, actually. I mean no guy has ever chased me, or wanted me like that. That would be too risky, you know like "deal or no deal risk".

"That spot on your forehead makes you look like a right Paki".

"So are you black or white?"

"Where are you from originally?"

Wiltshire.

"Ey?"

Oh yeah, sorry, Wiltshire's next to Somerset by the way.

"No, originally?"

Well I was born in Cambridge...

"No, *originally*, as in your dad?"

Oh, Africa.

"Whereabouts?"

Erm Kenya.

"Whereabouts?"

Ermmmmmmmmmm—

I am that mixed-race kid. You know the one you might see in town? You know the one, getting pushed in its pushchair by its white mum. And that kid has got some matted up, dried hair and dried-up skin.

I mean, it's kind of funny actually.

It's kind of flipping sad.

That being half black in an all-white area is a burden you wouldn't wanna have.

"Yes, yes, YES... but who are you?"

Confused.

"But who are you?"

That mixed up, the kid mixed up, myself mix up up, mix up me, trying to be white in a half-black body...

And

Still

Not

Enough.

I mean I straighten my hair and wear real light foundation.

So you can't say I don't try...

I try, I try, I try a lot.

And right now I'm really trying... I'm trying to look for a Shakespeare monologue for this stupid audition. But I can't pick one! Obviously because I can never decide on anything. I don't even understand Shakespeare, you know? And I don't even think I like it...so what's the point?! Why am I even trying...yeah so, forget London, forget drama school and forget this stupid monologue!

ROSE AND CROWN

BROGAN Ok ready Jaz? One... Two... Three.

JAZ *(JAZ takes a shot)* Down town, down Rose and Crown on Friday night...oh...God...no...that's...yuck!

BROGAN *(laughing hysterically)* That shot Jaz had your face like *(mimics)* you're like *(mimics again)*... Trust me you look well weird!!!

JAZ Coming from you! Miss "I'll just have the water please"... You've changed Brog!

BROGAN Whatever, Mitchell don't like it when I drink, so shut up!

JAZ Everyone knows everyone.

VILLAGER 1 Now I don't gossip I just heard from my boyfriend, nieces, brother—

VILLAGER 2 And I heard from my aunties, cousins, mother—

VILLAGER 1 Oh look, in he comes that Mitchell lad, ain't it sad about his brother getting paralyzed in Iraq...

VILLAGER 2 Yeah and that Brogan's just come in. God, she's such a slag...

VILLAGER 1 And she's dragged out that Jazmin friend of hers...

VILLAGER 2 Ohh that Jazmin, that Jazmin's all alone. Since her nutjob of a mum walked out of that home.

JAZ Around here the Rose and Crown is the place to be. But if I'm being honest, right now I'd rather not be here. It's just Brogan's got this new boyfriend called Mitchell and they've been going out—

BROGAN Seven weeks, thirty days, six hours, three seconds. Seven-and-a-half red roses a thousand kisses and NON STOP, rough, steamy, ORGASMIC—

JAZ She likes him a LOT. But more than a lot, she loves him, but more than love, he IS—

BROGAN "the LOVE OF my LIFE and I can't be without him Jaz".

JAZ Ever since they've started dating we've started chilling with him and his friends down the pub. And as much as I try... I just really, really don't like him.

BROGAN Isn't he just so funny?

JAZ No, yeah he's alright.

So like I said, I rather not be here. He's been talking for the last fifteen minutes...

MITCHELL Yeah, well the other day I went down town to get a curry. Now I was tired right cus I've been working all day. So I'm walking right, smoking a backy. I chuck it outside before I'm served by that Paki fella.

Anyway.

So I say to the guy, I say "I'll have a korma with chips on the side, yeah?!"

"Very good, sir."

So off he scurries to get my curry,

and three minutes later he's back with my meal in tow.

Now in that curry house they've got that seating area remember...? So I sit down there and dig in.

So there I am eating away, when all of a sudden I feel something...

Something on my tongue...

Now I ain't one to cause problems,

but it felt like a hair,

so there I am pulling out this big, long, greasy, black hair,

that fucking Paki's hair.

So I walk up to the counter with it in my hand like this *(shows audience)*

and say, "Excuse me, but I found this in my food, do you see this hair?"

And he looks at my hand, then stares me dead in the face and says,

"Sorry sir, I see nothing there".

So I say, "You don't see this hair?"

He says, "No".

I go, "But you can see me right?"

He goes, "Yeah".

I go, "Well can you see this?" and I pick up my Coke.

He's like, "Yeah".

All confused...

I go, "Can you see this?" and I pick up my curry.

And he's like, "Yeah."

So then, nice and slowly, I start pouring the Coke and the curry on the shop floor. And the whole time I'm just staring at him and staring at him, showing him not to mug me off!

And when it all runs out I say, "Now, do you see?"

And he's just like, "Yeah, I see clearly now".

And... Well...that's the end of the story really isn't it?

JAZ And the whole room is laughing.

So I start laughing.

She laughs.

Cus when I go to London right, I'm gunna have a real fresh start.

She laughs.

I'm gunna reinvent myself and grow myself.

She laughs.

The amount of people that I'll meet and all the things that I'll do, will outweigh the times I laughed and laughed and laughed, to get myself through.

She laughs.

I'll be drinking in a bar not a pub. Talking to new people not the same people. Being "someone" instead of "that one". And I'll feel proud.

She laughs.

But right now? Well, I'm just laughing aren't I?

And Brogan reaches over and gives my hand a squeeze,

cus I know that she sees,

but I'm embarrassed she sees,

that I'm embarrassed.

That she sees

that as they laugh,

I'm laughing too.

And the more that they laugh,

so do I do.

And I'm laughing and I'm laughing,

and I hate that I'm laughing.

It follows me home.

That laughing follows me

all

the

way

home.

It follows me home,

that laughing...

Until I open the front door...

And there in the kitchen, is my grandma on the floor.

GRAN

JAZ Gran—

GRAN *(inhale of breath)*

JAZ Gran!

GRAN *(inhale of breath)*

JAZ GRAN!

GRAN *(inhale of breath)* Yeah... I'm fine...love, fine...honestly, I'm—

JAZ Your heart!

GRAN Honestly I'm—

JAZ Let me help you up (GRAN *groans in pain)*
Gran you're in pain, I should have come back sooner.

GRAN *(inhale breath)* Love I'm—

JAZ You're fine, but you just don't look, don't seem, are you sure you're alright?

GRAN *(inhale of breath)* I've been rushing, doing too much, tripped on the...the...uh... *(pointing)*

JAZ The carpet Gran... We should call a doctor, give me one sec, I'll get you a doctor.

GRAN No Jaz. Jaz... Jaz, NO! *(Sighs)* I used to be a fighter.

JAZ What?! Are you joking me Gran? You still are.

But she's got her head hung like she's tired, like her fighting spirit has expired.

"What can I do Gran?" I say.

And I'm dusting her down, readjusting her crown. Her hand in mine.

"Things will be fine" I tell her and I'm scared. But I don't tell her that.

GRAN Have you been practising?

JAZ What?

GRAN Your monologue for the audition.

JAZ Oh Gran, that... It's not important right now.

GRAN How long have I been seeing you in plays?

JAZ Ermm, I dunno. Since I was five, you'd always come, you every time and never with Mum.

GRAN Just go for it, Jaz. Really, really just go for it. Promise me Jazmin.

JAZ I promise you, Gran.

Pause.

GRAN Well, go on then.

JAZ What?

GRAN Show me something then.

JAZ What, *now*?

GRAN Why not?

JAZ Gran we're sat here in like, pitch black.

GRAN Just for me love, show me a bit of your *(she breathes in with pain)*...ahh.

JAZ Gran you're still in pain... Look, I will ok, just promise me you'll breathe until we wait till the doctor gets here, ok, just breathe...

GRAN *(she takes an intake of breath)*

JAZ Breathe.

GRAN *(intake of breath)*

JAZ Breathe.

GRAN *(intake of breath)*

JAZ Sir spare your—

GRAN *(intake of breath)*

JAZ the bug which you would

GRAN *(intake of breath)*

JAZ fright me with I seek

GRAN *(intake of breath)*

JAZ to me

GRAN *(intake of breath)*

JAZ can life be no commodity

GRAN *(intake of breath)*

JAZ the crown

GRAN *(intake of breath)*

JAZ the comfort

GRAN *(intake of breath)*

JAZ of my

GRAN *(intake of breath)*

JAZ life.

Big intake of breath.

And I'm dreaming of the audience applauding, as I'm stood on stage recalling the times I prayed for this.

Intake of breath.

I pray for this.

Intake of breath.

And the lights are shining down. And the curtains are closing. And I'm searching for your face. But wait, I see it! I can see you Gran, you're sitting on the front row!

Intake of breath.

Standing ovation. You're smiling. Because you know.

Intake of breath.

We sat on the kitchen floor once and we dreamed about this.

Intake of breath.

"I'm sorry, Jaz, I'm holding you back."

You're not Gran, I'm here with you now, can't you see me?

Intake of breath.

Buzzing in this moment, I wish this feeling could last forever...

Intake of breath.

And out of all these people applauding,

I swear if my gran weren't here now, it wouldn't feel half as rewarding.

She's the only face I see,

as I'm staring at her and she's staring at me.

Ending on a few intakes of breath.

THE CHANGE

BROGAN Look, just relax, ok? Don't stress and if you do feel stressed then you should actually go and sit under our tree, you know? Trust me, just go up there, ok?!

JAZ Brog! That's not gunna help me, I don't have time!

BROGAN Tomorrow I promise I'll help you go over your lines. It's just I really want you to be here to celebrate me and Mitchell's eight-week anniversary.

JAZ I dunno Brog...

BROG Jaz, just for one night stop thinking sooo much about EVERY little thing. Sometimes you've just gotta fuck it all off and have some fun. Come on! Please Jaz. PLEASE!

JAZ So I have some drinks and a shot, drinking for this evening like it's the last night that I've got. And you know what? Things don't look so bad when you've had a few, I kind of like this distorted point of view. I'm happy momentarily which is better than not being happy at all.

MITCHELL "Jaz, take this, it will make you happy for as long as possible".

JAZ And Mitchell's handing me some little packet, with a little white tablet in.

BROGAN "Jaz what you doing? Don't do that! We don't do this, this ain't you!"

JAZ But Brog's so carefree...and messy thoughts don't hang so heavy on her mind. She feels wanted and who she wants is wanting her and...I'm lost in the deep blue of her eyes and her smile is beaming. I want that.

BROGAN "Don't take that."

JAZ *swallows the tablet.*

"I'll take it".

JAZ *starts spinning around.*

And I'm having fun! And I don't CARE!!! *(Says this whilst still spinning until she stops)*
Till I'm outside getting some air.
But who's spinning,
my head's spinning.
But who's standing over there?
St...st...staring...
I'm trying to see.
Eyelids feel so heavy,
vision moves unsteady,
but I swear spinning,
I swear that spinning,
I swear that's Mitchell,
inin
inin
spin
and he's, and he's...
blurring,
he's with someone.
I'm trying to see,
but what I see looks hazy,
and this spinning's going crazy,
but Mitchell's
head is spinning,
he's with someone.

Their bodies close, spinning, touching skin, spin, brushing skin

spinning, spin, spin.

I'm trying to move away,

cus I don't wanna,

can't and I

see him in this way,

with

and I can't

see him,

so I shan't,

so I'm moving

back...

back...

and...

Shit! Cus he's seen that I've seen and I know, what he knows, he's done. So I run, but he's got my arm.

MITCHELL You've been spying on me, watching me, you slimy piece of—

JAZ Ahhhh get off!

MITCHELL No you listen, you listen to ME!

JAZ I just came out for air, I wasn't trying to see—

MITCHELL SEE WHAT! You saw nothing and that's what you'll say, do I though? Do I though? Do I look—

JAZ Spinning

spinning

"I was just, I didn't mean to..."

MITCHELL Whatever you think you saw, you didn't see. No, NO you listen to me!

Suddenly the pub door opens and **BROGAN** *walks out.*

BROGAN Finally! Been looking everywhere for you two... Errm, what's going on out here? Everyone looks well serious. Jaz are you ok? You do actually look well shit mate... I should take her home.

MITCHELL She's fine Brog! Just them pills hit her bad, got her all confused not seeing things properly. Ain't that right Jaz...? RIGHT?!

JAZ Right.

BROGAN You sure? You just look really—

MITCHELL SHE'S FINE! Look just stay inside the pub with her until she's in the right frame of mind.

BROGAN That's true actually Jaz, cus you don't want your gran seeing you like this...

Wait, where you going?!

MITCHELL Gotta head off babe...got an early job tomorrow.

BROGAN But I thought you could stay?

MITCHELL Well I can make it up tomorrow. Listen take this...

He hands her some money from his pocket.

Last round on the bar so treat yourself to a few on me, and your little best friend too.

JAZ Let's just go, Brog.

MITCHELL You know, for someone so quiet, you really are fucking rude.

BROGAN BABE chill out! Of course we appreciate it like... Lots! Ok...well I guess I'll see you tomorrow then *(she giggles)* alright bye...bye... *(Giggles again, waits till he out of ear shot)* You could have at least said thanks and smiled Jaz! I mean, what's been going on with you tonight? You've been acting proper different.

JAZ Why do you like him?!

BROGAN Why are YOU so bothered? It's fucking weird Jaz! What? Do you want me to be single? Do you want me to be alone? Are you jealous?

JAZ NOO!

Yes.

No.

Yes.

NOOO, no I'm not—

BROGAN Then why can't you just be happy for me? Look, he's not this horrible person. That's just the version you see, but with me, he's well...sensitive. But you just don't know him like I know him, like I know, he had plans right to join the army, but he didn't pass his training. And yeah, I know, you know, you think you know, but no, I know him and I feel bad for him Jaz, cus he feels OBVIOUSLY shit, you know? But you don't. You don't know though! Cus you don't know him, like I know him, like I know. Every week he goes to the hospital his brother's at. And he'll just be sat in the waiting room for hours. I bet you didn't know that he's never gone in? And I know that, cus I know him as in know him and you don't know that cus why would you? When you don't know him like I know, like I know at night Jaz, when he thinks I'm sleeping I can hear him crying, like proper crying. And I know this, cus I know him, and you don't know that, cus you don't know him, like I know him, like I know, but I want you to know Jaz, cus I proper love him...you know? So what's your problem? Come on, what's your problem?

JAZ Go on then, tell her then, tell her then, tell her.

BROGAN Well?

JAZ Erm... Well... I dunno.

BROGAN See?!

JAZ Coward.

BROGAN Nothing to say.

JAZ Coward... *(To* BROGAN*)* It's just I really feel—

BROGAN Just stop now Jaz! Stop! I don't even wanna talk about it. Come on let's just go inside.

BROGAN *pulls* JAZ*'s arm back in the pub.*

FLASHING BLUE AND RED LIGHTS

JAZ The flashing blue and red lights are outside me and my grandma's house and I can feel myself—

POLICEMAN ...panicking. Please remain calm.

JAZ What do you mean remain calm? What's, what's going on? What happened?

POLICEMAN Are you the granddaughter?

JAZ Yes, yes, just tell me what's going on!

POLICEMAN Just calm down there ok... Breathe... Breathe... I just need to start by writing down your—

JAZ Flowers upturned, windows smashed, front door bashed in proper bad, but up...up on the side of the wall, words in red paint standing tall read... NI-GGER.

POLICEMAN Your name please?

JAZ NI-GGER.

POLICEMAN Your name?

JAZ And then it just clicks, I know who done this, I know who to blame. Mitchell, cus I saw him in that alleyway, so now he's tryna scare me not to say.

POLICEMAN Pardon?

JAZ What?

POLICEMAN Your name?

JAZ Jazmin... Jazmin Hunt.

POLICEMAN Jazmin we're taking your grandmother into hospital, she's quite poorly at the moment—

JAZ Flashing blue and red lights and this patronising policeman gives me a patronising smile.

POLICEMAN We've been trying to contact you for quite a while—

JAZ Are you the police or what?! How long does it take for you to tell me what's happening?!

I just wanna know if my gran's ok!

POLICEMAN Am I the...the police! I am in fact a very respected member of the village police with twenty years of experience! Look I can understand this must be quite stressful—

JAZ Ohhh my God! My gran's house has been smashed up. Obviously this is stressful!!!

POLICEMAN Lower your tone please! Lower your tone... We're just trying to assess the situation nice and slowly. Now can you think of anyone that might have ill feelings towards yourself or your grandmother that would be capable of doing this?

JAZ Mitchell.

POLICEMAN Annnnyone at all?

JAZ Mitchell.

POLICEMAN Nooooobody you can think of?

JAZ Coward. Coward. Coward. Coward... NO.

POLICEMAN OK! *(Speaking to himself as he writes on notepad)* Still...not...sure...who...the...suspect...is...follow...uhhh...oh this bloody pen... Chris have you got a spare—

JAZ Is my gran gunna be ok?

Blurring, blurring, robotic cold words are swirling from the policeman's mouth. I can't hear them, they run through me...

POLICEMAN Outside, on the floor, by the front door is where we found her. Climbed up the ladder she did, tryna wash the writing from the wall she was.

NIGGA. NIGGA. NIGGA. NIGGA.

Politically incorrect statement. She was tryna wash that

"GO BACK TO YOUR OWN COUNTRY"

before you got home. That's why she was rushing she was, that's why she fell she did. From the ladder, trying to get that deeply offensive PAKI racist term off the wall.

JAZ My gran.

POLICEMAN But we do have to inform you, her heart, we have to inform you, worst case scenario, we have to, be prepared, in a bad way, we have to, are you ok?

Are you ok madam?

JAZ And I'm not cus I just can't think of her not being ok.

But at the end of the day I promised her didn't I?

So I'm still gunna try,

so here I am trying to learn these—

sir, spare your

Nigg, Nigg, Niggling

I SAID, sir spare your—

"Alright my NIGGER?!"

The bug which you would,

the bug, bug, bugging me,

"What? They say it so why can't I fucking say it?!"

Sir, spare your—

Intake of breath.

The bug which you would

"Now I don't gossip"

Try again, the bug which you would—

I don't even understand Shakespeare you know?

Come on, for you, for me.

To me, can life be no PAK—

E, commodity!!!

Can life be no—

PAKI

"Now IIIIIIII

And I AM TRYING TO learn the lines but the words don't fit,

don't gossip."

I'm repeating these lines, but the words won't stick,

in fact there's not one bit of this monologue I actually like.

So think what you like, cus I not trying no more.

I'm dreaming of the audience applauding...

NO! I mean it! I'm not trying no more.

JAZ Let me catch my breath. Taken aback, the flashing blue
and red lights are blinding.

SURPRISE NEWS

In JAZ's *room.*

BROGAN It's a bit annoying to be honest Jaz, cus I just feel like your heart's not in it. And if your heart's not in it then don't waste my time!

JAZ Brog, bloody hell...

BROGAN Look, it's well crap that your gran's in hospital and it's even more messed up that some evil person did that to her house and I swear Jaz... I swear... If I could get her back home sooner I would. But you know what I'm like! I have to be honest. Sitting here, moping around your gran's house isn't gunna get you to London any sooner is it? And I ain't no "acting expert" but I know this Shakespeare wrote powerful words and you're about as powerful as a wet fish love, so try again alright... Alright?!

JAZ Ok... *(She prepares herself)* Sir, spare your threats the bug which you fright me with I seek. To me, life be no ahhhhh! Why did you do that?!

BROGAN Because I'm tryna make you feel something.

JAZ Yeah pain! You're making me feel pain Brog!

BROGAN Gooood! Try again.

JAZ Sir, spare your threats the bug which ahhhh! Brog, I swear to God.

BROGAN Jaz is your monologue happy?

JAZ No.

BROGAN Then what is it?

JAZ It's feeling... It's standing up to someone.

BROGAN *pushes* **JAZ** *hard so she falls to the floor.*

Brog you're taking this too far now...all I wanted was your help with lines.

BROGAN *(chucks a pen at her)* Stand up to me then! Come on... come on Jaz! *(Chucks more things in* **JAZ**'s *room at her)*

JAZ Look I don't have time for this, my audition is tomorrow and ahhh!

BROGAN Come on, what you scared of?

JAZ Just stop it.

BROGAN No.

JAZ Stop it.

BROGAN No.

JAZ Stop.

BROGAN No.

JAZ Ahhhh Sir, spare your—

BROGAN SHIT!

JAZ But I was just—

BROGAN SHIT!

JAZ Brog at least let me try, God! Sir spare—

BROGAN NAAAA.

JAZ Spare—

BROGAN NAAA.

JAZ SPARE YOUR THREATS, THE BUG WHICH YOU WOULD FRIGHT ME WITH I SEEK. TO

ME CAN LIFE BE NO COMMODITY. THE CROWN AND COMFORT OF MY LIFE, YOUR

FAVOUR. I DO GIVE LOST, FOR I DO FEEL IT GONE!

Pause.

BROGAN Oh my gosh mate...! That was well good. I felt something then.

JAZ I think I kinda... I think I felt something too... Shit what's the next line? Crap the line, Brog!!!

BROGAN I'm pregnant.

JAZ WHAT?!

BROGAN I'm pregnant Jaz, me and Mitchell are gunna have a baby.

JAZ But when, what?!

BROGAN I'm sorry I just can't hold it in. I'm seven weeks and I've been dying to tell you. I know it's fast...like really fast, but he's good Jaz and I'm gunna be a mum! I'm actually gunna be a mum!

JAZ But you haven't even been dating that long!

BROGAN I know but it just feels right.

JAZ Eight weeks you've been with him and it feels right?

BROGAN He loves me.

JAZ Does he?

BROGAN Yeah, he does actually! We've been try...well I'VE BEEN trying for a baby.

JAZ Wait, wait... So does Mitchell even know?

BROGAN No...

JAZ God Brogan! You can't do that... You can't just decide you want a baby with someone without THEM actually agreeing.

BROGAN Why you even being like this Jaz?! You know this is what I've always wanted! Why you turning this into some bad thing?!

JAZ Because it's just like... You don't know him Brogan!

BROGAN I know he loves me, I know I love him, I know... I know you don't go down to our tree no more, I know you don't put a rock down like you used to.

JAZ Well sorry Brog... I just don't have time right now to sit under some random tree with some stupid rocks ok!

BROGAN What's your problem!

JAZ It's just a lot... Can't believe you've known this whole time and never told me.

BROGAN Yeah well you never told me you might one day wanna leave here.

Pause.

JAZ So you're really pregnant?

BROGAN YES...! God!

JAZ ...Well... You're gunna be an amazing mum... Seriously.

BROGAN Finally! That's all I ever wanted you to say before.

JAZ I'm sorry Brog. It's just Mitchell, I really don't like him and—

BROGAN He said he loved me the other day Jaz and he said he can see a future with me, he said that to me.

JAZ Just with this audition... I can't leave my gran and I can't leave you Brog... I don't wanna leave you especially now more than ever...with the baby... I can't go.

BROGAN You drama queen! I am safe ok! And I know I take the piss, cus London people are actually really really aggressive... but if you get into this drama school you would make your gran so proud and I would actually be proud to be... like... "See that girl on EastEnders, well that's my baby's godmother".

JAZ You want me to be godmother?!

BROGAN Obviously *(laughs, pause)*

So let's go over your lines one more time then ok?

JAZ Ok! So when you gunna tell Mitchell then?

BROGAN Tonight...

JAZ I can come with you?

BROGAN No, no it's fine... Think it's better if I talk to him on my own.

JAZ Are you sure? I don't mind coming...what if he's not—

BROGAN He's gunna be fine Jaz. Stop worrying... Now come on let's get these lines done!

THE FALLOUT

JAZ Down town, down Rose and Crown.

VILLAGER 1 I don't gossip, I heard from Stacy's gran's, sister's son's, twin—

VILLAGER 2 And I heard from my hairdresser's half-brother's, friend of a friend's, ex-boyfriend, I heard it from him.

VILLAGER 1 Ohh... Mitchell and Brogan just come in.

You alright Mitchell? Yeah Brogan, Brogan! Alright Brog? You look lush babe, lush, don't she look proper lovely Sue?

VILLAGER Absolutely gorgeous love, yes you do Brog... She looked like a pile of—

VILLAGER 2 Shit they're fighting again.

Mitchell does treat her proper bad.

VILLAGER 1 And how he speaks to her, proper sad... Well pass me the crisps it was just getting juicy.

VILLAGER 2 You see they're heading outside.

VILLAGER 1 Great... *(Eats crisps)*... It was just getting good.

VILLAGER 2 Debbbb! You know that half-cast girl?

VILLAGER 1 Oh yeah, the same one that I heard don't wanna stay here no more. She ACTUALLY wants to go places she's never been before.

VILLAGER 2 Yeah, that one.

VILLAGER 1 Jazmin she is.

VILLAGER 2 Well she just come in—

VILLAGER 1 Quiet Sue she's coming over—

VILLAGER 2 What?

VILLAGER 1 *(in an exaggerated murmured tone)* SHE... IS... COMING OV—

JAZ Hi, sorry I just wondered have you seen Brogan around here?

"Outside" they reply, with their judgmental stares and a small-minded eye. "Thanks" I say, as I make my way round back.

VILLAGER 1 Oh and by the way how is your gran love? We heard she's not doing too good?

JAZ And they do really good concerned facial expressions and makes noises like "hmmm", "ohhh". And the truth is, I know they couldn't really give a crap, so I continue to make my way round back. Don't even wanna be here really, but Brog might need me, clearly she does... Take a step round back and—

MITCHELL Well what do you want me to say?! *(He shouts in her face, aggressive body language)*

BROGAN I dunno, I dunno, that things will be ok. *(Crying)*

MITCHELL What the fuck are you doing here? *(Seeing JAZ appear)* People like her will bring you down, did you plan this?

BROGAN No babe I swear I didn't know she was coming!

MITCHELL You're lying to me!

BROGAN I'm not I promise, I told her not to come.

MITCHELL And you wonder why I don't want this baby with you.

BROGAN *(crying and more distressed)* ...Right... Right, I'm going.

MITCHELL You go when I say you can go.

JAZ And he's got her up against the wall with his hands around her neck.

BROGAN Jaz!

MITCHELL You best keep out of this, you hear that, get away!

BROGAN Jaz!

MITCHELL She ain't coming for you, she ain't been there for you.

JAZ Glued to the spot can't move.

And I'm scared, I wish I could be brave but I'm moving back, getting away.

STAY.

But I can't.

BROGAN Jaz! *(Gasping for air)...*

JAZ And I'm staring at her,

and she's staring at me,

I hate that I'm staring I hate that I see.

Her nose is running, her makeup is smeared, her face is blotchy red

and she's still beautiful to me.

I wish I could save her,

I really wish I could.

And she's staring at me like "Just this one... This one time, I wish that you would."

BROGAN *tries to catch her breath as he lets her go.*

Watch him walk back in the pub and Brog are you ok?

BROGAN *is still catching her breath and is bent over in pain... She takes her times before she replies.*

BROGAN Why... Why did you come here Jaz?

JAZ I wanted to be here for you.

BROGAN And what did I say? Go on!... Go on! What did I say?!

JAZ You... You told me not to come.

BROGAN That's right! I told you not to come because you just make things worse. And even when you are here you don't... You don't even help. And now you're standing there crying like you're some little kid. Grow up Jazmin!... And leave me alone, go on, go... I said go! Are you deaf? Fucking go! ... Stop standing there. GO!... GO!

JAZ But I don't go, cus I can't and I won't let go. And Mitchell starts talking loud, standing in the middle of the crowded pub addressing the whole room like he's the grand finale of a show we've paid to see. Standing there just a couple feet from me... shouting bout niggers and pakis like this is his last act, cus he knows the only mixed-race girl will never react. He says...

MITCHELL So I'm in Co-op yeah, and this PAKI is with her pack of kids. And one of the little shits runs into my bad knee.

JAZ And

the room

is

laughing.

MITCHELL So I say "Oi control your pack of kids yeah, they're behaving like animals!"

JAZ And the laughing

grows louder.

MITCHELL And this PAKI actually tries walking away, so I follow her and then she says "No English, no English."

JAZ And louder and louder...

MITCHELL So there I am in Co-op, walking after this PAKI, with her pack of kids and I say "Then why are you in England if you can't speak English?"

JAZ Standing there thinking how can you possibly define a race with your own ignorance?

MITCHELL And the Paki's shaking as she's walking. Dropped her shopping as she's walking.

JAZ And I'm bubbling as he's talking, cus I'm struggling to hold my tongue.

MITCHELL And I walked that Paki and her pack of kids right out of Co-op I did! I did! And if I could walk that Paki and her pack of kids right out this country I would. If I could get rid of every single one of those, those—

JAZ PAKIS!

MITCHELL What?

JAZ Just can't be scared any longer,

have to be stronger,

I can't hold it in,

the room's silent and—

MITCHELL What?

JAZ Pakis, that's what you wanted to say right?

MITCHELL Yeah... So anyway, if I could get rid of every single one—

JAZ OF THOSE PAKIS!

MITCHELL SHUT UP!

JAZ Make me!

BROGAN Jaz what the hell!

JAZ That's me. I'm that Paki, I'm that Chinky from the fish and chip shop, I'm that tanned-looking, half-cast, terrorist.

MITCHELL *(laughing louder)* She's lost it now... Watch her go... Watch her!

JAZ Don't come near my gran, don't come near Brogan.

BROGAN Jaz, what's got into you?! *(To* **MITCHELL***)* Babe I swear I don't know what she's talking about, just stop this Jaz, stop joking around.

JAZ I'm serious, I'm actually really deadly serious.

MITCHELL *laughing even louder.*

MITCHELL Oh no!!! She's deadly serious now, watch me mate I'm actually shaking.

JAZ They're laughing sounds heavy.

Like every time I laughed when the joke was on me.

BROG Let's just relax ok? I think Jaz is just going through a lot right now... Right Jaz?! Right?!

JAZ And I can see Brog's panicking, the room's listening and I'm tired of holding back.

Mitchell...didn't you try and join the army once? But you couldn't even pass training—

BROGAN Jaz STOP!

JAZ God! It must be draining, failing like you do. Acting like you're something, but we all know you're broke. And yeah you keep laughing, keep laughing, cus it is funny. You are a JOKE! And the punchline is?

BROGAN Jaz please!

JAZ You go to the hospital your brother's at. But in reality you're sat in the waiting room week after week. And you know how I know that right? Cus at night... She can hear you crying, so stop pretending, stop fucking lying. You are—

BROGAN Jaz stop this, this ain't you!

JAZ You're that retching before sick, you're the push before the shit, you're the blow to the hit, you're ignorant meets thick, and you know it! You believe what I say and you're own self-hate makes you bitter in every type of way.

BROGAN For me Jaz! FOR ME!!!

JAZ Go on then, tell her then, tell her then, tell her.

BROGAN Leave it.

JAZ You...

BROGAN Leave it leave it.

JAZ You...

MITCHELL *(clearly embarrassed he tries to cover up with laughing)* Alright. Ok. I hear what you say. Let's just leave it, yeah? We'll leave it at that. Agree to disagree, accept my apology, whatever you want love, whatever makes you happy.

JAZ What?

MITCHELL Is there much else to say or are you done?

JAZ And he's smiling at me like real calm, like he's done tryna cause any harm.

And I think of Gran, she's telling me

"I REALLY believe you can do it Jazmin".

Turning around, heading towards the door.

MITCHELL Half breed.

JAZ I feel my eyes sting and tears welling *(breath)* that hurt, don't let myself cry *(breath)* but that hurt.

She turns around to face him.

And the whole room is laughing hard and I'm trying hard not to cry and that's when my best friend Brogan catches my eye.

She's just stood there just staring at me.

And I'm staring at her like "Brog help".

But she's watching me,

like I watched her,

and didn't help.

And I'm staring at her,

And she's staring at me,

And the whole room's laughing,

except for she

and I.

Her eyes stare at me, real sad and pitiful, belittled,

I'm crippled in her gaze.

She's almost amazed at how scared I am

and I am

but I can and I will make you proud Brog.

I'm gunna show ALL them how strong I can be,

I'm gunna let them know you can't take the piss out of me.

And I will make you proud Brog,

even if the rocks we collected smash into your dreams

even if the tree we sat under is not as magical as it seems.

Cus I don't care, broke down, tired and I'm stripped

and the one thing you taught me is never ever quit

on your dreams.

So I'm chasing after mine,

and I hope that in time you'll understand why I'm throwing these—

Half breed is it? Half breed! I bet you've been gagging to say that like a piece of phlegm needs to be spat. Yeah, you've been waiting on it, choking on it, like food in lodged—

MITCHELL Na I just say it like it is because the truth can't be dodged.

JAZ Truth, do you really think you're being truthful to everyone in here Mitchell?

MITCHELL *(laughs)* What?

BROGAN Babe, what she talking about?

JAZ I slowly pick up a rock from under me and Brogan's tree...

"Tell them the truth Mitchell."

MITCHELL You're fucking mad!

JAZ "The truth is, deep down you're just like me and that scares you."

I throw it and watch it ricochet back.

MITCHELL Shut up, right! Shut up!

JAZ So now I take a bigger rock and I throw it again.

"Tell them what I saw?"

But again it ricochets back.

MITCHELL I'm warning you right, you better—

JAZ "Tell the truth! Who I saw you with and what you were doing."

And now I take the biggest rock from me and Brogan's tree and I'm about to smash up everything.

BROGAN Just stop Jaz!

JAZ But it's too late, cus I've launched it and now this huge rock is just flying

through the air.

"Cus I saw you with that guy and you were,

kissing on"

Flying.

MITCHELL Shut up!

JAZ "Kissing on."

Flying.

MITCHELL Shut up. Shut up!

JAZ "Kissing on—"

MITCHELL Shut up.

JAZ "Kissing on—"

MITCHELL Shut up.

JAZ Flying, flying, flying, flying, flying, flying, flying, flying...

"YOU WERE KISSING ON HIM!"

And the rock I've thrown has shattered everything and the shards coming down are painful.

Pause.

But I don't care!

Because I swear this tree is dead and these rocks never meant shit. But I'll miss it, I'll miss it, I'll miss every single bit.

Every single stone, every tower of rocks we've collected, I'm just pushing them down, over and over and over again. And I don't stop till I see the roots from me and Brogan's tree uplifting causing the ground we've always stood on to start shifting.

And all our rocks are crumbling, there tumbling down around us,

I watch our tree come crashing down, so I set it alight. I know it's not right.

But now it's in flames.

I know I'm to blame.

"I'm sorry" I mouth that to Brogan, but I don't know if she can see me, cus all our rocks are falling down.

"I'm sorry" I say, "I'm sorry", cus I want her to know that I am. But she's just clutching her belly as her dreams fall heavy to the ground.

And she's still staring,

and the rooms still spinning with the rocks I've been flinging

but all I can see is her.

And I've got to get away, I can't stay.

So I start running, I run out the pub and I don't know where I'm running to but I'm running and suddenly I realise I'm running to my favourite place, the only place, I feel safe... me and Brogan's tree. And when I get there I see more rocks then I've ever seen before, and they've all been rearranged and placed on the floor and it reads...

"CHASE.UR.DREAMS"

"CHASE.UR.DREAMS"

Spelt from all the rocks me and Brog have ever collected and more. And I'm just standing there, tears rolling down my face, cus I realize now...why Brog's been telling me over and over again, to go back to our tree and I've just ignored her...or been too busy, or frustrated because "I don't have time to sit under a friggin tree with rocks Brog".

Forgetting,

forgot.

I'd forgotten... That this is where we go, were we've always gone...to find faith and Brogan's been trying to give that to me this whole time... I just didn't even realize.

"CHASE.UR.DREAMS"

I'm running.

And I think of my gran,

"I really believe you can do it Jazmin".

"CHASE.UR.DREAMS"

And I think of Brogan.

I'm running.

I'm running...

FINAL

And I'm running, running, running, eyes streaming and I'm running so fast, praying that I'm running past all this mess. Running past stress, running past pain, running from my own self-blame, running from my gran being sick, running past Mitchell and every individual who has ever judged me, running from Brog and her baby, running towards something that will save...

Sir, spare your threats

The bug, which you fright me with, I seek

You don't intimidate or deter me, you don't scare me, you can't put me down. Stronger than your hate it's faith that I've found.

I am barr'd like one infectious.

Outcast like the half-cast I am.

Healed out to murder, myself on every post proclaimed a strumpet.

Half breed, half-cast, nigger, Paki, Chinky, puff, queer, bent, faggot, gayyyyy boyyyyy, you slut, slag, whore, spastic, retard, pikey, gyppo, inbred, immigrant, **SCUM!**

But

I have got strength of limit.

Strength that is bigger than me, more than I could have fathomed, more buried then I could see.

Yes I'm half breed, and sometimes I hate the fact I'm half black and half white, I hate the fact you stand on and rip up any culture in your sight. Most of the time I'm guessing I'm never completely sure on anything, I'm just chasing something better.

But hear me when I say... Apollo be my judge

cus I know,

one day,

I'm gunna go further than this village, and when I do come back,

you,

you'll be stood outside Co-op,

you'll be rolling a backy

and you'll still be talking shit about us niggers and Pakis.

THIS
IS
NOT
THE
END